Roman Corbridge

Fort, Town and Museum

Nick Hodgson

CONTENTS

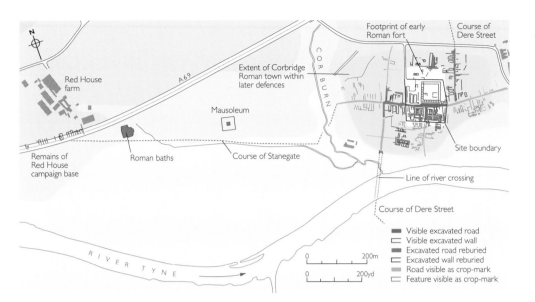

Tour of the Site

OVERVIEW AND SETTING

Roman Corbridge lies among cultivated fields on a gently rounded elevation above the river Tyne, some 25 miles inland from the North Sea. To the south the ground falls steeply to the river, while to the north it rises gradually towards Hadrian's Wall, 2.5 miles distant and out of sight. The Cor Burn valley offers protection to the west, and half a mile beyond it is Red House farm, where a Roman campaign base was briefly occupied from about AD 77 to AD 85, before a fort was built at Corbridge. To the east, beyond a dip, the Saxon church tower of the modern town of Corbridge can be seen less than half a mile away.

The site commanded the junction of two main Roman roads: that running north–south between Scotland and York (named Dere Street by the Saxons), and the 'Stanegate', running west–east from Carlisle (its easternmost point is not certain). Dere Street bridged the Tyne immediately west of the site and the southern bridge abutment can be glimpsed (on the other side of the river) when the waters are low. Massive blocks from the road ramp leading onto the bridge, saved from river erosion in 2004, have been re-erected close by. Just south of the bridge a branch road probably led south-west via Allendale to the remote fort at Whitley Castle, which supervised lead-mines near Alston.

The visible remains of Roman Corbridge represent only a small fraction, the nucleus, of the later Roman town. The entire site (still extant, though levelled by agriculture) is known, from air photographs and the pre-1914 excavations, to cover roughly 40–50 acres (15–20ha) of the surrounding fields. It was enclosed by defences in the later Roman period.

Above: Map of the Corbridge area. The first Roman campaign base was at Red House, west of the main site; the modern town is to the east (not shown). Buried remains affect the growth of vegetation above, producing 'crop-marks', as shown on the plan, that trace the remains below

Below: The Emperor Vespasian (r. AD 69–79), depicted on the obverse of a coin of AD 75 found at Corbridge. It was under Vespasian's rule that the first campaign base at Red House was occupied

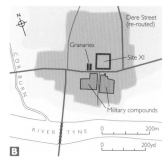

Above: The development of Corbridge

A The mid second century AD; when the fort was still in use

B About AD 200, Corbridge now a legionary supply base surrounded by a fully developed town

C The late Roman period, showing the conjectural line of the new town walls

Above: Builder's tools found at Corbridge – an adze-hammer, plumb bob and mason's trowel

Below: Detail of Trajan's column of c. AD 113–17, showing legionaries building a fort. They would have used tools like those above

The succession of early forts, deeply buried and largely invisible beneath later remains, faced south, with their headquarters at the centre of the present enclosure. When the last of the forts was replaced by a town in about AD 160, Dere Street was adjusted to dog-leg through the centre of the town. Anyone travelling north to the Wall, or Scotland, had to go east along the main road, the Stanegate, before turning north again beyond the modern enclosure.

Today the Stanegate forms one of the most recognizable landmarks among the remains. It separates the vast courtyard building known as Site XI, a fountain, and the granaries (on its

north side) from the complicated remains of the two legionary compounds to the south.

Corbridge has many layers of archaeological deposits, which record successive stages in the Roman history of north Britain: from the forts, begun as a springboard to further conquest to the north, to the legionary bases supporting the new permanent frontier that was Hadrian's Wall, to the fully grown late-Roman town that reflects the economic development of the province and the emergence of a regional capital for the civilian population of the eastern Wall area.

▣ *PRINCIPIA* (HEADQUARTERS) OF THE FORT AND ▢ *PRAETORIUM* (COMMANDER'S HOUSE)

The central area of the fort lies north of the Stanegate. It was later covered by the large courtyard building, Site XI (see page 6), which belongs to the town and legionary supply depot that replaced the fort. On the west side of the open courtyard, however, part of the north range of the *principia* of the last fort is still visible. The main surviving structure is its square shrine (*aedes*). The vertical slots in its inner wall faces show where originally a timber structure stood, before being

Left: *Reconstruction of Corbridge fort as rebuilt in about AD 142 to support Antoninus Pius' Scottish invasion. Roman fort commanders (prefects) had to prepare for winter conditions like this, as we hear from a Vindolanda writing tablet where a prefect orders goods in October to allow his men to 'endure the coming storms even if they are troublesome'*

A *Principia* (headquarters) of the fort

B *Via principalis*

C *Via praetoria*

D *Via decumana*

E Barracks

F *Praetorium* (commanding officer's house)

G Baths

H Military annexe (conjectural)

I The Stanegate

J Dere Street

K Civilian houses and workshops

L Bridge over the Tyne (position at this date conjectural)

M The Cor Burn

Above: A Roman officer sacrificing at an altar, detail of a slab that marked part of the Antonine Wall built by the 2nd Legion, c. AD 142
Below: Remains of the square shrine of the principia of the last fort

Below: Aerial view of Site XI
A Shrine of the fort headquarters
B House of commanding officer
C Entrance to courtyard building

encased in stone. The attached curving wall to the south dates from after the end of the fort, when the area was used for metalworking. About 20m to the east the foundations of the *praetorium*, the house of the commanding officer, of the last fort can be seen. These fort structures were never fully cleared away because the later courtyard building was never finished.

Main Roads of the Fort

The Stanegate follows what was one of the main roads through the fort, the *via principalis*, which connected the east and west gates. The road between the two legionary compounds south of the Stanegate follows the line of the *via praetoria*, leading south from the *principia* to the main south gate of the fort (*porta praetoria*). The successive forts have been only fragmentarily seen in narrow excavation trenches dug through the strata of the later town, so their exact sizes are not known, but the west rampart of all but perhaps the earliest fort lay along a line where the museum stands today, and the east rampart lay just within the fence-line of the site.

❸ COURTYARD BUILDING (SITE XI)

This great courtyard building (known since its discovery in 1908 as Site XI) lies north of the Stanegate: a square of some 66m surrounded by ranges. The entrance, with underlying drain, is in the centre of the south range, which was divided into rooms opening onto the Stanegate. The west range is divided into square rooms with openings of about 4m onto the courtyard, suggesting shop fronts.

Most of the masonry has gone, taken for building material over the centuries, but what remains are striking: massive

blocks, tightly jointed and surmounting a fine moulded plinth. The block faces are heavily rusticated, with bosses left projecting from the smoothly drafted margins where the blocks had to fit flush against one another. The quality and scale of the craftsmanship indicate an important imperial building project, although its purpose remains unclear. It has been suggested it was intended as the forum for a new city or a *principia* of a new legionary fortress. It is closely paralleled in plan, however, by store-buildings at Continental legionary bases and by certain markets in Rome, so it is likely that it was a storage and marketing centre supplying the forts along the frontier.

Abandonment
The south range of the courtyard building was completed and used, but the rest was abruptly abandoned, unfinished. The court was never fully levelled and the upper blocks at the north end of the east range remain undressed, their surfaces never smoothed to take the next course of masonry.

The construction probably began in the 160s or 170s and there are several possible crises that may have caused its abandonment, including the emergency of the Marcomannic Wars on the Danube in the later 160s and an attested crossing of Hadrian's Wall by invaders in the early 180s.

Above left: Remains of the wall of the south range of Site XI. The masonry blocks fit precisely against each other, while their outer faces are heavily rusticated
Below left: Remains of a row of bases for the columns that supported shop porticoes opening off the south range of Site XI onto the Stanegate; the street drain can be seen to the right
Below: Open-fronted shops would have surrounded the open courtyard of Site XI, perhaps similar to this cloth merchant's shop depicted in a Roman relief of the second century AD

Below: Black Burnished ware bowl, manufactured in the Thames Estuary area and used as tableware during the life of the forts at Corbridge

The Corbridge Hoard

In 1964 archaeologists digging down to the early forts deeply buried beneath Site XI came across the disintegrated remains of a chest made of alder wood, bound with iron and covered in leather for waterproofing. It contained a hoard of military equipment, tools and other items. The chest was buried during the first half of the second century, probably during the life of the second or third fort.

Among the contents were parts of at least six cuirasses of plate armour. Although heavily corroded, these remains are the best preserved ever found of the famous armadillo-like segmented plate armour (*lorica segmentata*) as worn by legionaries depicted on Trajan's

Column and elsewhere. The Corbridge find showed for the first time how the armour fitted together, allowing the definitive reconstruction that can be seen in the museum.

The presence of plate armour at Corbridge may indicate that a detachment of legionaries was present during the fort phase, but such armour may also have been used sometimes by auxiliaries.

Other objects from the chest, some displayed in the museum, include spear and javelin heads, catapult bolts, a pickaxe, chisel, saw, shears, crowbar, knives, a pulley-block and miscellaneous items ranging from a horse harness and gaming counters to textiles, rope, feathers (possibly

for helmet plumes), and, rarest of all for Britain, papyrus.

The hoard shows that parts of worn, damaged and previously repaired cuirasses were being assembled in a workshop awaiting further repair and reuse. Possibly they were concealed with other useful items when some or all of the unit was transferred from the fort, expecting to return. Whatever fate befell the hoarders, they never recovered the chest.

Left: Reconstruction drawing of the chest and its contents

Below: Some of the contents of the chest buried at Corbridge

A Bronze military fitting, exact use unknown

B Leaded bronze chair leg decorations

C Bronze cuirass tie-hook

D Fragment of papyrus

E Wooden fragment of writing tablet

F Bundle of spearheads, knife, iron bar and chisel, bound with rope

G Bronze military belt plate decorated with enamel

H Lead bowl

I Iron spearhead with ash shaft

J Iron knife with bone handle

K Iron pickaxe head

L Iron lamp and lamp bracket

M Tankard of wooden staves and bronze, with single handle

N Iron shears

O Iron pulley block with part of its wooden pulley wheel intact

P Slide key

Q Iron saw, with fragments of cloth and wood attached to it

R Glass melon beads

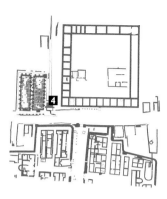

Above right: Fragments of the fountain pediment bearing a wreathed inscription held by two Victories
Below: Remains of the substructure of the aqueduct channel that brought water to the fountain
Bottom: The large drawing tank of the fountain, facing onto the Stanegate

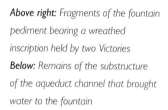

4 FOUNTAIN HOUSE

Between Site XI and the granaries to the west is an elaborate fountain, built in the later second or early third century as the main public water supply for both legionaries and civilians. The fountain gave life and sparkle to stale aqueduct water by cascading it into an open tank and from there into a public trough – an arrangement found in countless Mediterranean cities but rare in Roman Britain.

An aqueduct channel brought the water from a source (unknown today) to the fountain head via a covered stone conduit that enters the site 70m north of the fountain. As the conduit approached the fountain it was raised on a stone-faced substructure to maintain a sufficient head of water. The whole, conduit and base, was encased in a clay bank, surviving as a grass-covered mound. The conduit and all but the very base of the substructure have been removed by stone-robbers.

The aqueduct embankment ended against a wall facing the Stanegate. Only the lowest part survives, but it would once have formed a decorative screen, hiding the utilitarian mound behind it. In front of this screen was a structure housing the spout, framed between columns and topped by a pediment.

Its rectangular foundation survives and fragments of the pediment, which commemorates the 20th Legion (see page 38) as builders of the fountain, can be seen in the museum. The water dropped some 1.3m from the spout into a large hexagonal aeration tank. Its slabbed floor, which remains, is founded on a platform of blocks originally held together with metal or oak cramps. Grooved stones for the upright panels of the tank can be seen at the front and the west side.

From the aeration tank the water spouted into a large drawing tank fronting onto the Stanegate. The slabs forming the sides have been worn away, in places almost to the level of the base, an effect common in Roman public troughs caused by people leaning over with buckets, washing clothes, and sharpening implements. This tank was a replacement of an original whose floor can be seen projecting slightly to the west. It was probably from the south-east corner of the earlier tank that an outflow ran across the Stanegate to supply tanks in the street between the legionary compounds. The fountain is flanked by statue bases (later additions). Plough marks on the eastern base indicate the pre-excavation ground level.

Above: Reconstruction of the fountain at Corbridge. The east granary can be seen to the left

Below: Bronze jug found at Corbridge. The fountain would have provided a constant supply of fresh water for drinking, cooking and other uses

Roman Water Supply

'With such an array of indispensable structures carrying so many waters, compare, if you will, the idle Pyramids or the useless, though famous, works of the Greeks'.
Sextus Julius Frontinus (Governor of Britain AD 74–7), from his Aqueducts of Rome

Major settlements – forts and towns – were supplied with water by aqueducts, which brought water from sources often many miles distant. Most people think of Roman aqueducts raised in part on arches, but such structures were rare in Britain. Here public building was on a modest scale and water was usually conducted over long distances in an open channel following the natural contours with a very slight gradient.

After impurities had been deposited in settling tanks at the point of arrival, gravity distributed water along systems of water pipes, which might be of timber, lead or tile. Ceramic pipe sections were made with a constricted end to fit into the next piece, and the joints were made watertight with mortar. The Corbridge lion (see page 33), which started life as a funerary monument, was adapted to act as a fountain gargoyle fed by such a piped water supply.

Rainwater collection tanks had sides of stone slabs slotted into grooved pillars or joined with tongues and grooves. They were sealed to make them watertight with lead or mortar.

Underground and surface drains made of timber or stone took storm water, tank overflows and waste water out of the settlement, often designed to flush out communal latrines on the way. At Corbridge these conduits led towards the slope down to the river.

Above: The Corbridge lion. It was probably carved in the second or third century as a funerary monument but adapted to form a fountain

Right: Examples of the 'indispensable structures' of Corbridge

A Drain from the water tank within the west compound. It joins the drain in the side street running down to the river

B Water tank in the side street for the east compound. It was fed by an underground channel from the fountain on Stanegate

C Arched culvert through which the drain **A** joined that in the side street

D West compound water tank. The surviving side slab is worn down at the top by use

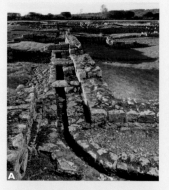

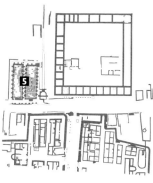

Left: The column bases of the granary porticoes fronting the Stanegate
Below: A legionary reaping grain; from Trajan's column, Rome, c. AD 113–17
Bottom: The granaries, as built probably under Severus in AD 198–209

5 GRANARIES

The granaries are the best preserved of the standard military type anywhere in the Empire. The remains visible today are of those probably built under Septimius Severus (r. AD 193–211): an inscription of AD 198–209 from a granary, reused in the crypt at nearby Hexham Abbey (see page 46), is likely to have been taken from one of these buildings.

To keep the contents of these two grain stores cool and dry, the floors were raised on dwarf walls above a ventilated basement. Buttresses supported the thick outer walls. In front of the doors facing onto the Stanegate were loading platforms (only the eastern one survives) covered by porticoes. The impressive portico column bases can be seen at the edge of

Above: A surviving mullion in one of the ventilators in the east wall of the east granary
Below: Looking north along the east granary. The dwarf walls that raise the flagged floor from the ground to provide ventilation can be seen clearly

Facing page top: The west granary from the north. The smooth flags of the raised floor on which the grain was stored are well preserved

the road. All except the outermost eastern bases were raised in the late third or early fourth century when the Stanegate was rebuilt at a higher level. By the late fourth century the road had risen far above the granary entrances, which now had to be reached down a set of steps.

East Granary

The east granary stands higher than the west. A decorative chamfer (bevel) 1.8m above ground level survives halfway along the outer west wall, showing that the thickness of the wall and buttresses was reduced at this level. The flagged floor is less complete than in the west granary, so the substructure of dwarf walls can be seen more clearly.

A row of pier bases, built as one with the basement walls, runs the length of the centre of the granary, probably to support an upper floor. In the east wall one of the ventilators still has the stone mullion that blocked access to the basement.

West Granary

The west granary contains the remains of a predecessor with its floor at a lower level. The earlier and lower system of dwarf walls, packed solid, is best seen at the south-west corner and running crosswise from inside the north-west corner. This earlier granary probably belongs to the legionary supply depot of the 160s, when a walled compound (still partly visible) surrounded the granaries. All earlier work in the east granary was obliterated by the Severan rebuild of AD 198–209.

Repairs and Inscriptions

Ian Richmond (see page 48) found an even earlier system of walls (not visible) in the 1940s. He attributed these to the granaries of Fort IV (AD 139/40), which are commemorated in magnificent inscriptions naming Quintus Lollius Urbicus, Governor of Britain AD 139–42, found reused as flooring slabs in the granaries remaining today and now in the museum.

Also found reused were several religious sculptures now in the museum (such as the Jupiter Dolichenus frieze and the sun god panel; see pages 32 and 26 respectively). They were found in the loading bays and floors, part of repair work of the fourth century, when these cults were no longer followed.

Coins found here in considerable numbers show that the granaries were still in use in the late fourth century, by now operated by the civil authorities, who collected tax in the form of grain and maintained a food supply for the townspeople.

Above: Partial relief of a winged horse from the pediment of the temple to Jupiter Dolichenus. This fragment was found reused in the east granary
Below: One of two inscriptions naming Quintus Lollius Urbicus found reused as paving in the granaries

Below: Mortarium, gritted mixing bowl, stamped by the potter Sulloniacus, dating from the time of the last fort

SOUTH OF THE STANEGATE

The remains of the two military compounds south of the Stanegate appear at first as a confusing mass of walls. But their enclosure walls are recognizable: unusually wide (1.3m) and following a winding course that carefully excludes certain buildings, not forming part of the compounds, which front onto the Stanegate at the east and west ends of the site. The outer face of the compound walls is shown by the decorative chamfer (bevel) on the second course above the ground (see photograph opposite). Two parallel depressions that run east–west through the compounds are the result of part of an earlier fort (before AD 163) – possibly a street, cambered so that its centre was raised. Buildings later constructed over this street have sunk into the subsiding ground on either side.

The compounds housed legionary detachments (each of about 100 to 200 men, from a mother unit of over 5,000) based at Corbridge in the third century. The respective *principia* of the compounds faced each other down the long vista formed by the central east–west street, suggesting that the two compounds were laid out as part of one overall plan. This axial street now forms the southern edge of the current site; the southern half of the military compounds remains buried in the fields beyond.

❻ EAST COMPOUND

Most of the area south of the Stanegate was excavated before 1914, but Ian Richmond re-examined it in 1936–43 and it was he who recognized the enclosures as legionary compounds. His identifications of the various buildings have mostly been accepted ever since, but some are open to question.

❼ Shops Outside the Walls

At the east end of the site four plots front onto the Stanegate. Three have foundations of massive, crudely worked blocks, and the compound wall skirts around the back of all four plots, which led Richmond to identify them as the *podia* (bases) of temples. There is rich evidence for cult activity at Corbridge and Richmond reasoned that only sacred buildings would have been respected by the compound wall. But the block construction was common in civilian buildings in the frontier area. The buildings were probably commercial premises or official stores and were left intact for the essential role they played, like the granaries and Site XI, in military supply.

West of these buildings, cobble foundations show how the east compound wall was originally set back from the road to make room for further commercial premises, with a 4.4m wide projection to accommodate a passage to a side-gate squeezed between shops on the street frontage. Later the compound wall was moved out to the edge of the Stanegate.

Above: Shops and stores probably lined the south side of the Stanegate outside the compound walls. A merchant is shown selling foodstuffs in this third-century relief from Ostia, Italy

❽ East Compound *Principia* (Headquarters)

The eastern wall of the east compound runs inside the modern enclosure fence. Just within the eastern wall, in the south-east corner of the modern enclosure, are the poorly preserved cobble foundations of the *principia*. It is very small, suitable for a detachment rather than a full unit: there is no colonnaded

Below: The massive base of the east compound enclosure wall. The second course of stonework is angled to form a decorative bevel on the outer face

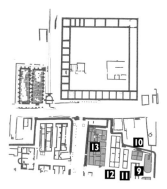

Below: Tombstone of Marcus Favonius Facilis, a centurion of the 20th Legion in the first century. A detachment of this legion was at Corbridge by AD 160. The east compound houses were probably built for legionary centurions

Bottom: The east compound barracks, seen from the south-east corner

courtyard, merely a long, narrow hall backed by an apsidal (semicircular ended) shrine flanked by offices. The *principia* commands a view down the east–west axial street to the compound entrance 40m away and, beyond it, to the *principia* of the west compound.

9 Meeting Rooms and 10 Granary

Behind the *principia* are remains of two apsidal buildings. Richmond thought these were *scholae*, meeting halls for the unofficial religious associations (*collegia*) of soldiers in the Roman army. The smaller building may have been a shrine.

North of the *principia* is a rectangular structure divided into four with underfloor channels (not now visible). The channels connected to still-visible ventilation openings in the outer walls, suggesting that this was a granary. Reports from the Edwardian excavations (see pages 46–7) show a similar building on the south side of the *principia*, outside the fenced area.

11 Workshops, 12 Barracks and 13 Officers' Accommodation

West of the *principia* are two rectangular buildings north of the axial street. The smaller was probably a workshop, the larger a barracks, but its layout is not fully understood. Further west a 3.5m wide street runs north at right angles.

Complex remains lie to the west of this side street. Originally these formed two houses. Each was roughly 50 Roman feet square (14m²), with an entrance corridor and seven rooms ranged around a central court. Presumably they accommodated officers in charge of the legionary detachment, centurions rather than more senior equestrian officers to judge by the relatively small size of the houses.

The house to the north was entered from the side street, the house to the south from the main axial street, just inside the east compound gate. At some point these two houses were converted into one larger building. The west and north

Left: Fully armed legionaries on the march; from a detail of Trajan's column in Rome, c. AD 113–17

Below centre: Dedication slab found at Corbridge. It bears an inscription of a century of the 6th Cohort (a subsection of a legion) and a depiction of a boar, the symbol of the 20th Legion

Roman Legionaries at Corbridge

The ranks of the legionaries contained trained craftsmen, explaining the quantity of high-quality religious sculpture and architectural stonework found at Corbridge.

The soldiers stationed along the Wall and at the early forts at Corbridge were mostly auxiliaries: non-citizens initially recruited from the enemies Rome encountered on her frontiers and later from Rome's provinces. The Roman citizen troops were organized into the famous legions, heavy infantry units some 5,000 strong. By the second century legionaries were increasingly recruited from citizens in the Mediterranean provinces, rather than Italy.

After AD 122 the legions of Britain were based in fortresses at York (*Legio VI Victrix*),

Chester (*Legio XX Valeria Victrix*) and Caerleon, near Newport (*Legio II Augusta*). Frequently *vexillationes*, or detachments, were split off from their legions on special duties or to assist campaigning armies.

Legionaries were needed in the area of active frontier warfare far north of the legionary fortresses and, after AD 160, Corbridge was permanently home to two detachments from different legions. An inscription dedicated to *concordia*, or harmony, between these intensely proud detachments suggests that rivalry existed. No doubt fights broke out between these two units – one reason why in the third century they occupied separate walled compounds.

Bottom left: A legionary holding a standard topped with an eagle into whose beak Victory puts a wreath; from a slab marking the building of part of the Antonine Wall, c. AD 142, by a detachment of the 20th Legion

Below: Flag of a detachment of the 2nd Legion; relief probably from the west principia at Corbridge

A sculptured panel probably originally from the west compound *principia* shows the *vexillum* (flag) of a detachment of the 2nd Legion, and other stone panels depict legionary standards of the kind seen on Trajan's column.

Above: The southern of two houses
that probably served as living quarters
for centurions in the east compound

A Entrance to east compound

B East–west axial street

C Original entrance to house

D Tank, for industrial processes in
later Roman times

E Purpose unknown

Above: Pottery sherd from Corbridge,
depicting a smith: metalworking was
one of the principal activities of the
legionary base and town

Right: Iron tools found at Corbridge

A Slater's hammer

B Small saw

C Wedge, marked with initials
(probably those of its owner)

D Leather-working awl

E Carpenter's chisel

sides were extended, lining the inner face of the compound wall. Later the compound wall was removed (probably by post-Roman stone robbers), leaving the rough core of the walls of the building visible today.

The overall purpose of this larger converted building is unclear. Two rooms opening off the enlarged northern court have broad thresholds, 2.75m and 2.15m wide, which were closed with double doors, suggesting it was used for storage. A room in the north-west corner has a heating system, indicating it was a living area. At some stage industrial activities were carried out here, including pottery: two tanks full of unworked yellow-red potting clay were found in what was the north-east room of the southern house, and in the next-but-one room was a pottery kiln, represented now by an uneven platform. None of the coarse yellow-red ware evidently made here has been identified in the site collection.

Other changes can be traced in the compound, notably walls superseding the buildings north of the *principia*. In the late third and fourth centuries all the legionary buildings must have been replaced, or their uses changed, to suit the needs of the late-Roman inhabitants, whether military or civilian.

14 SIDE STREET TO THE COMPOUNDS

Beyond the drastically robbed main gate of the east compound is a street that runs north, at right angles, towards the Stanegate, perpetuating the line of the *via praetoria* of the fort, and separating the legionary compounds. The north end of this street was blocked off to the public when the east compound wall was extended to the edge of the Stanegate.

Originally two towers flanked a gate from the Stanegate to the side street; the remains of the towers can be seen as projections from the extended compound wall. On either side of the street is a water tank (one for each compound), each fed by a conduit running beneath the Stanegate from the fountain on its north side. Drains on both sides of the street carried overflow to the river; one is joined by an outfall from an arched culvert through the west compound wall.

15 WEST COMPOUND

The west compound gateway is as badly robbed as that of the east compound. It leads west, in a mirror of the east compound, onto the east–west axial street and on to the *principia*. Just north of the gate the compound wall incorporates a small rectangular building with a western apse and two entrances. The plan suggests a temple or shrine that clearly pre-dates the compounds: it must have originated in the legionary supply depot of the AD 160s. Although incorporated into the west compound, the east entrance of the temple opens onto the street between the compounds and so was accessible to soldiers from both legionary detachments.

16 West Compound Barracks

Two rectangular barracks 20m long, run at right angles to the axial street. Each was originally formed of a back-to-back pair of buildings, each of these some 10 Roman feet (3m) wide

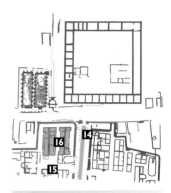

Above: The apse of a small temple built in the AD 160s and later incorporated into the western legionary compound

Below: The west compound from the gateway to the Stanegate
A Remains of one of the towers of the Stanegate gateway
B West compound water tank
C Conduit feeding tank from the Stanegate fountain
D Side street drain
E Temple
F Barracks (later workshops)

inside, and separated by a stone party wall running the length of the block. At both ends are projecting wings that perhaps served as stores or offices. The positions of doorways suggest that each half of each building was divided in half again by a central timber partition.

Although only two of these back-to-back pairs are clearly visible, the compound had five. They are much smaller than typical fort barracks, which held a century of 80 men. Each one of these paired barracks at Corbridge would only have accommodated about 32 men, the five in total housing a detachment of perhaps 160 legionaries.

The pre-1914 excavations found many furnaces, tempering tanks, and much iron slag in these buildings, leading Richmond to identify them as the workshops of a legionary depot for the repair and manufacture of weaponry. These activities in fact belong to the later third or fourth century, when the buildings were no longer all functioning as barracks. There are signs that their plan was much altered in this later period: the front walls were moved out to align with the fronts of the projecting wings, and many new partitions were inserted.

Facing page top: Relief found in the west principia *strongroom of Hercules raising a club to strike the Hydra (missing, except for a tentacle wound about Hercules' arm). Minerva (left) directs his blow*

Facing page bottom: The altar to Discipulina, *dedicated by the 2nd Legion, found in the west* principia *strongroom. Discipline was observed not merely as a duty, but as a cult by soldiers in the Roman army*

Below: The strongroom within the principia *of the west compound. The steps led down from the shrine room*

🔟 West Compound *Principia* and Strongroom

Further west along the axial street is a water tank on the right and then, straight ahead, the *principia*. Like that in the east compound, this headquarters building has a compact design, but its layout is highly unusual. In place of a transverse hall, the front part of the building was divided by arches into three bays, each entered by one of three doors in the façade. The central bay rose higher, lit by a clerestory, like a church nave with flanking aisles. This 'nave' led to an antechamber giving access

'Military exercises have, in a way, their own rules: if anything is added or removed from them, the exercise either becomes less useful or too difficult. You performed the most difficult of difficult exercises, throwing the javelin while wearing the cuirass … I also approve of your spirit.' Address given to the 3rd Augusta Legion in North Africa in July AD 128 by Hadrian, who is shown on the coin below addressing (no doubt in a similar vein) the EXERC[ITUS] BRITANNICUS, the 'Army of Britain'

to the shrine of the standards and to offices on either side, to the north and south. A flight of steps led down from the shrine room to an underfloor strongroom beneath the southern office, once barrel-vaulted, where the unit funds were kept.

The side offices had openings onto the bays at the front of the building which were closed off by counters and grilles, like an old-fashioned bank or ticket office. Here the soldiers could get their pay.

Finds from the *principia* displayed in the museum evoke its brightly coloured shrine packed with altars, statuary and standards: the altar to the discipline (revered as the goddess Discipulina by the military) of the joint emperors (uncertain which ones) found cast into the strongroom, and a panel from a series depicting the labours of Hercules. The *principia* was later much altered: a range of rooms was added on its north side, including a hypocaust still in use in the late fourth century.

Towards the museum, the west compound wall skirts around a series of rectangular buildings. As in the east compound, these are unlikely to be temples, as Richmond believed, but were probably commercial premises engaged in military supply on the Stanegate frontage. In this area the contents of a pottery shop which had been destroyed in a fire while still in use were excavated in 1907.

Corbridge Museum

OVERVIEW

The Corbridge finds form one of the largest and most impressive collections of Roman objects from Hadrian's Wall. They fall into three main groups: those from the pre-1914 excavations (mostly concerned with the late Roman town), those from the work of 1947 onwards (which explored the early forts on the main site), and those found in 1956–7 and 1974 (at the earliest military base at Red House; see page 35).

Outstanding in the museum is the Corbridge Hoard (see pages 8–9) and the inscriptions and sculpture from the religious cults of the legionaries based here in the second and third centuries, found in the pre-1914 excavations. These stones survived in such numbers because they were reused, when the cult temples were pulled down after AD 370, to repair buildings and resurface the Stanegate. Other notable finds are now in the British Museum or the collection of the Society of Antiquaries of Newcastle upon Tyne in the Great North Museum.

Above: Remains of amphorae at excavations at Corbridge in 1909
Below: The tombstone of the four-year-old Vellibia Ertola from Corbridge, shown playing with a ball

Facing page: Reproduction of the Corbridge Lanx (see page 45)

GLIMPSES OF OTHER LIVES

Hundreds of tools and small objects give a vivid picture of everyday life and work, but some inscriptions give precise insights into the lives of particular individuals.

The Granary Officer

An officer proud of his assignment to oversee the Corbridge granaries at the time of 'the most fortunate British expedition' (during Septimius Severus' Scottish campaigns of AD 208–11), erected an altar in front of the granaries where he fulfilled his busy role (see box page 44). The word for granaries on the inscription is *horreorum*.

Barathes, the Standard-bearer

A gravestone records the death of Barathes, a *vexillarius* (cavalry standard-bearer), aged 68, far from his birthplace in the desert city of Palmyra in Syria. He may have settled at Corbridge after his discharge. Barathes is a common name in Palmyra and a namesake recorded at South Shields was probably a different man.

Two Little Girls

We have few individual names from the later Roman town, but gravestones identify two little girls. Vellibia Ertola 'led the happiest of lives for four years and sixty days' according to the inscription by her father, Sudrenus (see page 33), while Ahtehe – a Germanic name – lived to the age of five. The very un-Roman names of these people are typical of the Celtic and Germanic populations of the northern frontier.

Above: Two rare, gold openwork rings found at Corbridge: that at the top (a replica, the original is in the Great North Museum) bears the inscription in Latinized Greek 'Aemilia – long life to you!', and that below a love-token given to, or perhaps by, Polemius

Facing page top: Dedication dating from AD 162–8, to Sol Invictus, the Unconquered Sun, which originally adorned a temple to this god

Facing page right: Relief of a pilaster bedecked with roses from a panel probably once in the west principia

Love and Long Life

Two rare gold openwork rings naming individuals have been found at Corbridge. The museum displays a replica of one, with the inscription in Latinized Greek, *Aemelia zeses*, 'Aemilia – long life to you!' a formula that may indicate that Aemilia was a Christian. The other, now in the British Museum, is inscribed in Greek, *Polemiou philtron*, 'The love-token of Polemius'.

INSCRIPTIONS – SIGNPOSTS TO HISTORY

In the absence of other records, inscriptions are the only means of dating events at Corbridge precisely. The letters cut into the stones would have been painted red, and relief decoration and sculpture was also brightly coloured.

Two building inscriptions of the emperor Antoninus Pius are displayed with the missing parts restored. They are dated by the emperor's consulship ('II COS' and 'III COS') to AD 139 and 140. Both mention the governor Quintus Lollius Urbicus. The panels probably adorned the stone granaries of the final fort. They were found cut down and reused as floor slabs in the granaries visible today. The elaborate detail of the *peltae* (shield-like motifs) and other carvings surrounding the inscriptions (in one case upright acanthus leaves alternating with lotus flowers) is typical of the mid second century.

Very fragmentary, but also restorable because of the standard formulas used, is a large slab with magnificent lettering of the joint emperors Marcus Aurelius and Lucius Verus, dating to AD 163 or 164. It records building work by a detachment of the 20th Legion (see page 38), and so marks the transition of Corbridge from an ordinary fort to a legionary supply depot. It must have come from a large building, not now identifiable.

Oriental Cults at Corbridge

Below: Third-century relief of the sun god Sol, found reused as a floor slab in the east granary. It formed part of the decorative iconography of the temple to Jupiter Dolichenus

The cult of Jupiter Dolichenus merged the Roman god Jupiter with an all-powerful sky god originating in Asia Minor. It coexisted with the worship of Jupiter alone, and of other merged versions of Jupiter and was popular throughout the Roman army.

There is rich evidence for this cult at Corbridge, where several reliefs from a temple to Jupiter Dolichenus survived reused in later Roman work. They include a frieze of Sol, the sun god, flying on a winged horse towards one of the Dioscuri, the heavenly twins (Castor or Pollux), attendants of Dolichenus, and deeply incised panels of Sol and one of the twins leading his horse. The panels may have fronted a bench for reclining at ritual meals.

There is evidence, too, for several other cults with origins in the eastern part of the Empire. From AD 160 the legionaries built a series of classical temples (see

Of the same period, recording Calpurnius Agricola as governor of Britain, is a dedication to Sol Invictus (the Unconquered Sun) that would have adorned an undiscovered but clearly substantial temple to this deity. It was built by a detachment from the 6th Legion (see page 38), showing that by the 160s two legionary detachments were involved at Corbridge. The dedication is also flanked by *peltae*. Adjacent panels would have depicted winged Victories: their hands can be seen grasping the *peltae* on the central stone. The whole was some 5m long. At the top is a lewis hole, a slot used to attach the stone to a crane that lifted it into position.

Another panel fragment, undated, shows the *vexillum* (incorrectly inscribed 'vexillus'), or flag, of a detachment from the 2nd Legion, flanked by fluted pilasters. One is crowned with roses in reference to the May festival *rosaliae signorum*, when the standards of Roman army units were worshipped and bedecked with roses. This panel and others showing standards with roundels attached to a pole may have lined the walls of the shrine in the west compound *principia*, where the altar to Discipline dedicated by the 2nd Legion was found.

page 40), the appearance of which can be reconstructed from ornate architectural fragments (not on display in the museum) found reused in a fourth-century resurfacing of the Stanegate. One was dedicated to Sol Invictus (the Unconquered Sun). The temples have not been found, but probably stood in an enclave that may have included temples to other oriental cults of which evidence remains: Panthea-Cybele, the great mother goddess, and Astarte and the Tyrian Heracles, both worshipped according to mysterious occult rites at the Syrian port of Tyre. It is possible soldiers brought these cults with them when they returned from service in the war against the Parthian Empire fought in the east in AD 162–6.

The altars to Astarte and Tyrian Heracles (now in Carlisle and the British Museum) are inscribed in Greek, the language of the Eastern Empire, and name a priestess, Diodora, who practised at Corbridge.

Above: *Second- or third-century Roman bronze from Germany depicting Cybele, the mother goddess, one of several deities of eastern origin worshipped at Corbridge*

27

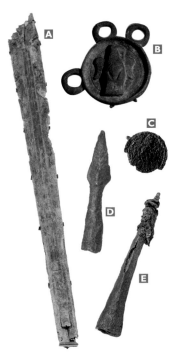

Above: Roman military equipment found at Corbridge

A Bronze scabbard

B Soldier's bronze strap junction decorated with an eagle

C Bronze button decorated with red and green enamel

D Iron spearhead

E *Pilum* (javelin)

Above right: Detail of the 'Bridgeness' slab marking completion of part of the Antonine Wall by the 2nd Legion. A cavalryman is shown riding in triumph over barbarians, AD 142–3

ARMS AND ARMOUR

The Corbridge Hoard (see pages 8–9) display, gives details of the discovery and contents of the hoard. Most notable is the cuirass or suit of body armour with interleaved iron plates and plated shoulder guards. One half is the original Roman material and the other is a modern reconstruction. The reconstructed plates were articulated on the inside using a system of metal hooks and leather straps; the evidence for these can be seen, much corroded but unmistakeable, on the Roman half.

Buried with the armour were the metal parts of various weapons, many displayed here, showing something of the range available to first- and second-century soldiers. There are *pilae* (javelins with a tip that bent and hooked into an opponent on impact), numerous spearheads and spear ferrules (ring to prevent the spear shaft from splitting), and bolts for firing from mechanical catapults.

The Horse at War

Remains of horse tack are often found on Roman sites where cavalrymen were stationed. Corbridge has examples dating from the early forts, *c.* AD 86–160. The first garrison at Corbridge was the *ala Petriana* cavalry unit. A cast of the tombstone of Flavinus, standard-bearer in this unit, is in the museum (original is in Hexham Abbey; see page 34) and gives a good idea of what cavalry horse tack looked like.

Far left: Reconstruction of horse's head protection, or chamfron, from remains found at Newstead fort

Left: Horse's bronze eye guard found at Corbridge, from the time of the first fort, *c.* AD 86–105. It would have been stitched into a leather chamfron

EVERYDAY LIFE IN THE TOWN
Health and Beauty

Personal items, mostly from the third- and fourth-century town, give an idea of the appearance of the people of Corbridge at that time. There are hairpins, combs, rings, bracelets, a fragment of a silver mirror, a make-up palette, and brooches for the fastening of cloaks, tunics and dresses. One delicate silver pinhead takes the form of a hand holding a fruit. Cosmetic implements, such as probes and tweezers, and small glass perfume flasks suggest that physical attractiveness was as important then as now. There are also medical instruments that would have been used by doctors practising in the town.

Home and Leisure

Coins, locks and keys, oil-burning lamps and candlesticks for homes and workplaces evoke the environment and activities of the townspeople. Many were literate, judging from the large number of *styli* (pens for inscribing wax tablets) found on site, and seal-boxes (writing-tablet packages were tied closed, the knot covered in wax and impressed with the sender's seal by encasing it in the little seal-box, so that the recipient would know at once if the tablet had been opened in transit).

Board games were popular among soldiers and civilians. A gaming board, counters and dice, of a type found all over the Roman world, are on display. Remarkable as this collection is, it represents only what survived in the ground. Most of the fabric of everyday life – textiles, foodstuffs, wooden objects, documents – has decayed and is lost to us.

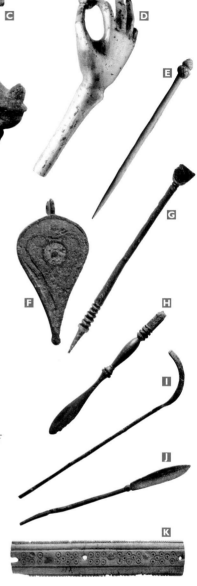

Above and left: Roman personal items

A Pottery oil lamp bearing the boar, the symbol of the 20th Legion, *c.* AD 86–105

B Bronze enamelled candlestick

C Bronze enamelled cockerel

D Silver pinhead in the form of a hand holding a fruit

E Bone pin

F Bronze enamelled seal box

G Iron stylus

H Bronze scalpel handle

I Bronze cosmetic/medical probe

J Bronze cosmetic/medical scoop

K Fragment of bone comb

L Gaming board, dice, counters and dice shakers

Right: Red Samian-ware bowl. Samian ware, made in Gaul and common across the Empire, was used at Corbridge until the third century
Below: Coarse fawn-coloured ware such as this was produced for everyday use by the army in their own kilns at the early forts at Corbridge
Bottom: A 'hunt cup', produced in the Nene Valley, near Peterborough, in the third century

PRODUCTION AND SUPPLY
Pottery

As bulk traded goods such as textiles and grain rarely survive, understanding of patterns of trade and supply relies largely on pottery. Samian ware from Gaul – the lustrous red pottery used throughout much of the Roman Empire – was traded from the Continent to supply the troops at the early Red House base, the early forts, and the town until the third century. A number of complete vessels were found at Corbridge and several of the various standard forms are on display – often bearing a tiny stamp with the potter's name.

For more everyday use the army at first produced coarse grey, fawn or ochre-coloured wares in its own kilns, but by the time of the later forts, from AD 120 onwards, the northern frontier was supplied from industries in southern Britain (so-called Black Burnished ware 1 and 2). Both the early coarse ware and the Black Burnished ware are well represented in the museum, as are grit-studded grinding bowls (mortaria) for foodstuffs and medicine. Some of these mortaria were made in northern Britain, some apparently at Corbridge itself, and others were traded from southern centres such as Colchester (identifiable by the leaf-shaped maker's mark), and from Gaul.

In the third century the import of Samian ware stopped and, as the economy of the province developed, the northern frontier became dependent on supplies of pottery from production centres within Britain that exploited the gap in the military market. These included the Nene Valley, near Peterborough, which produced colour-coated beakers. Fine examples of Nene Valley 'hunt cups', showing hounds at the chase, are on display. By the fourth century the pottery industry near Crambeck in Yorkshire dominated supply: a painted pipeclay Crambeck vessel found at Corbridge is one of the latest types of pottery to be found in Roman Britain.

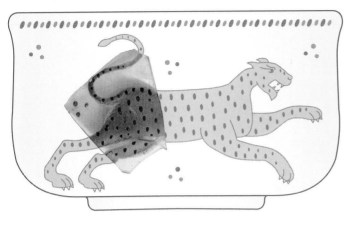

Glass

Glass finds are rarer because, unlike broken pottery, glass was a valuable material that could be recycled. But Corbridge has an impressive collection. Most of the vessels would have come from the Rhineland, but a fragment of millefiori glass (in which glass rods are fused together for ornamental effect) and the cast-and-polished bowls may have come from Italy, or even Alexandria in Egypt. On display are a flagon, flasks (notably the complete blue one for bath oils, see page 1), square bottles in various shapes and sizes, perfume flasks, and beakers and jugs. A painted fragment depicting the haunches of a leopard is a survival of a distinctive type of bowl from a Cologne workshop which was supplying northern Britain in the late second or third centuries. These small cylindrical bowls were painted with scenes from the arena. Other similar fragments are engraved with fishes, letters and palm branches.

Tools of the Trade

The museum gives a good sense of the industrial and economic activity in the late Roman town. Masons' hammers and trowels and a carpenter's chisel are on display. There are crucibles and various tools used in metal-, leather- and woodworking. Pottery was produced (on a relatively small scale) in the third century – evident from kiln furniture and several sherds of appliqué-decorated grey ware vessels. One such vessel has the maker's name – Assetio – and some have a figure of a smith in relief, an allusion to the metalworking that must have been prevalent in the town. A clay mould for such an appliqué figure shows a god with a wheel and a crooked club; the labourers on the pre-1914 excavations called him 'Harry Lauder' after the contemporary music-hall entertainer whose stage-prop was a twisted walking-stick.

Above left: A finely painted fragment depicting the hind legs of a leopard. This type of bowl was imported to northern Britain from Cologne

Above: The remains of a similar bowl from Cologne, found at Vindolanda fort just south of the Wall. It shows gladiators in combat

Below left: An almost intact flask of the late first or early second century

Below: An impression of an unknown god with a wheel and a crooked club, made from a mould found at Corbridge. The moulds were used to decorate pottery

Above: Remains of the third-century frieze from the temple of Jupiter Dolichenus, depicting the sun god Sol on the left riding his horse Pegasus towards one of the Dioscuri, Castor or Pollux, and a garlanded colonnade

Below: Statue, probably of Juno, dated from the hairstyle to the third century

Below middle and right: *Altar inscribed with a dedication to Jupiter Dolichenus, Juno Caelestis and Salus by Caius Julius Apolinaris, centurion of the 6th Legion. Its left side panel depicts a cupid carrying grapes, a combination symbolizing fertility and prosperity*

RELIGION AND DEATH
Honouring the Gods

The larger altars on display, such as that put up by soldiers of the 2nd Legion to Discipulina (Discipline), were dedicated by the military. They also erected much of the impressive collection of religious sculpture, such as the temple pediment to the goddess Roma, showing Romulus and Remus, and a frieze from a temple of Jupiter Dolichenus (see box page 26). Particularly impressive is a richly decorated altar to Jupiter Dolichenus dedicated by a centurion of the 6th Legion, who identifies Brigantia, the goddess of the northern region, with Juno Caelestis, the Syrian consort of Jupiter Dolichenus.

Also in the museum is a copy of the remarkable 'Corbridge Lanx' (see page 45; the original is in the British Museum). This silver dish, found in 1735 on the banks of the Tyne, just over half a mile downstream, depicts the worship of Apollo on the island of Delos in the Aegean. Probably from the same hoard as the lanx was one of the few Christian objects found in the area of Hadrian's Wall: a silver bowl decorated with the chi-rho (also now in the British Museum). It indicates that pagan traditions and Christian belief coexisted among the well-to-do of the fourth-century town.

The Corbridge Lion

A highly accomplished sculpture, the 'Corbridge lion', found in 1907, was part of a funerary monument in the second or third century. The fierce, human-like eyes of the lion stare at the viewer while he crouches over his prey: a lifeless stag, or perhaps a goat.

The group symbolizes the destructive power of death, and tops a coping stone that originally capped a wall surrounding a high-status tomb. The stone was later reused as a fountain in a large house (sometimes known as the *mansio*, an inn for official travellers, but there is no evidence for this), overlooking the river south of the west compound.

A hole made for a water spout destroyed the lion's bared teeth. A second, extremely weathered, lion came from the enclosing wall of the mausoleum at Shorden Brae (see page 40).

Below: The Corbridge lion, probably dating from the late second or early third century. The lion's original bared teeth were drilled away to fit a water pipe

Local Influences

Reliefs, figurines, portable shrines and several other small objects indicate the everyday beliefs and superstitions of the townspeople. Many reliefs and votive figurines, some in a Celtic style, were found of Mercury, a god associated with trade and commerce. A Celtic god, Arecurius, known nowhere else, is shown in a high-quality sculpture, where he is given a classical guise. There are many carved stone heads in the Celtic tradition (see page 44), more than at any other site in the north, a sign that the beliefs of the indigenous population continued to have a place in the town. A small bone leg was probably a votive to be offered to the temple of a deity in the desperate hope that a leg ailment would be cured, or in thanks that it had been.

Honouring the Dead

Tombstones found reused in buildings and repair work in the late Roman levels of the town centre would have been brought from cemeteries that lay outside the town. Among them are the gravestones of Barathes, the veteran soldier, and the child Vellibia Ertola (see page 25), who is shown, playing with a ball, in a local style far removed from the classical tradition. A row of holes below her figure may have held hooks for hanging garlands.

Below: Second- or third-century relief of Mercury, the god associated with trade and commerce and with the underworld. He holds a caduceus (wand) in his left hand and a bag of money in his right. A goat crouches at his feet

History of Corbridge

BEFORE THE ROMANS

It is now known that lowland Northumberland was largely cleared, settled, and cultivated by farmers centuries before the Roman invasion. The Roman name of Corbridge, apparently the *Coria* recorded in writing tablets found at Vindolanda fort 12.5 miles to the west, means 'hosting place' in Celtic, suggesting a meeting place or centre for the people of south-east Northumberland and the Tyne valley. The name of this Celtic people is unknown.

There was a pre-Roman building at Corbridge, although whether still occupied when the Roman army arrived and founded the first fort is not known. Beneath the remains of the forts, at the centre of Site XI, archaeologists found a circular gulley in 1952. They thought it a palisaded enclosure, but it was probably the drainage gully around a timber roundhouse nearly 14m across, with a south-west facing entrance. A smaller circular structure, probably of an earlier period, lay within.

THE ROMANS ARRIVE

The Roman army first penetrated Northumberland in the AD 70s, a generation after Claudius invaded southern Britain in AD 43. Anti-Roman forces took over the pro-Roman regime of Queen Cartimandua, ruler of the northern Brigantes, in AD 69, after which the Romans resumed their advance northwards under the Emperor Vespasian (r. AD 69–79). The governor Julius Agricola (in Britain c.77–83) set out to invade Scotland and complete the conquest of the island; it was this that led to the first Roman military activity at Corbridge, a key position on the invasion route east of the Pennines.

The first Roman occupation was over half a mile west of the present site, at Red House farm, where Roman baths were found in 1955. Buildings associated with a fort, explaining the presence of the impressive baths, were found during the construction of the A69 bypass in 1974. Too little has been excavated to know much more than that it was a large and important military base of Agricolan date.

Agricola's decisive victory in Scotland at the battle of Mons Graupius (AD 83) seemed to complete the conquest of Britain, but a series of barbarian invasions on the Danube frontier rapidly led to the withdrawal of troops from the island and consequently a retreat from most of Scotland. Agricola's son-in-law, the historian Tacitus, complained that 'having been thoroughly conquered, Britain was immediately thrown away'. Units fell back, dispositions were reorganized, and by AD 86 there were no Roman forts left farther north than that at Newstead, on the Tweed.

'He learned the rudiments of war in Britain … gaining a knowledge of the country, making himself known to the army, learning from the experienced, and imitating the best' Tacitus writing c. AD 98 of Julius Agricola, one of whose victories in Britain is the likely subject of this coin of AD 79, showing Victory standing over a captive

Below: Bust of Vespasian, under whose rule the first fort was built at Corbridge; from central Italy, c. AD 70

Facing page: First-century tombstone, now in Hexham Abbey, of Flavinus, standard-bearer of the ala Petriana cavalry unit, who 'lived 25 years, served 7'. He is shown mounted and armed, triumphing over an abject Briton

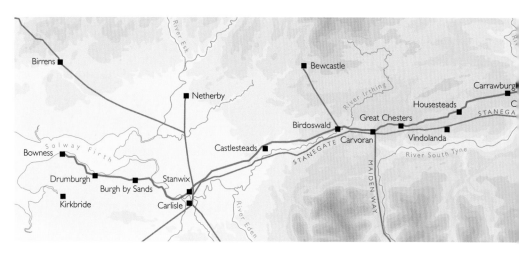

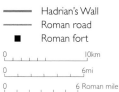

——— Hadrian's Wall
——— Roman road
■ Roman fort

0 ————————— 10km
0 ————————— 6mi
0 ————————— 6 Roman mile

CORBRIDGE: A NEW FORT

It was probably at this time of retreat from the north that the Red House base was abandoned and the fort moved to the main site at Corbridge, which perhaps offered a better point for the newly engineered Dere Street to bridge the river Tyne.

The remains of the succession of forts buried beneath the later town were explored from the 1940s to the 1970s in narrow, disconnected trenches between the walls of later structures, giving only a fragmentary picture of the layout of the early forts, especially of the earliest (Fort I).

Fort I was founded in about AD 86. It was built of timber, with posts set in trenches over a metre deep. Its overall size is not known, but it may have been larger than the later forts. Among the buildings are a possible *principia* (headquarters), a granary and a building with rooms opening off an aisle (once thought a hospital, but more likely a workshop or store).

The first-century tombstone of Flavinus (see page 34), standard-bearer of the auxiliary cavalry unit *ala Petriana*, was found only 3 miles away at Hexham. It suggests that this elite cavalry regiment, 500-strong at the time, garrisoned Fort I (and possibly the earlier Red House base). Correspondence on the Vindolanda tablets show that Corbridge was an important centre in the AD 90s: soldiers from Vindolanda were detached here and came here on leave; the commanding officer at Vindolanda, for example, the prefect Flavius Genialis, was invited here to visit his colleague Haterius Nepos, probably commander of the *ala Petriana* (see inside front cover flap).

THE EARLY SECOND CENTURY

At the beginning of the second century further wars on the Continent meant troops were again withdrawn from Britain. There were severe military setbacks in the north. In about AD 105 Corbridge was burnt down, possibly by enemy action. North of the Tyne–Solway isthmus, on which Corbridge lay, all forts were abandoned. A new fort was built at Corbridge as part of a new frontier line ('the Stanegate frontier').

Below: Haterius Nepos writes from the new fort at Corbridge inviting his colleague, the commanding officer of Vindolanda, to visit him; fragment of one of hundreds of discarded writing tablets of the AD 90s found at Vindolanda fort

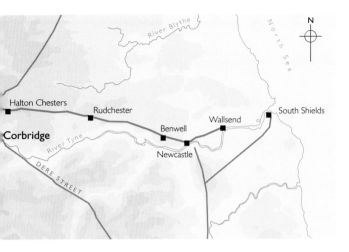

Left: Map of Hadrian's Wall, which ran for 73 miles across northern Britain. Corbridge, which pre-dates the Wall, lies 2.5 miles to its south
Below: Bronze portrait head of the emperor Hadrian (r. AD 117–138). It was found in the river Thames in 1834
Bottom: Part of the Wall today. It was built under Hadrian from AD 122. Originally it was 4–5m high, and remains today about 2.5m wide

The new frontier line meant that the new fort (Fort II) occupied a key position. Its buildings, enclosed within a turf rampart, were again of timber, and again of post-in-trench construction. The fort was playing-card shaped and faced south, covering 6.7 acres (2.7ha). Its east and west sides have been found, coinciding with the east and west sides of the modern enclosure, and its east–west road (*via principalis*) between the side gates ran on the line of the Stanegate visible today. Immediately north of this road lay the *principia* and granaries. Another road (*via praetoria*) ran from the front of the *principia* to the south gate. Barracks lay north and south of the central buildings. The name of the garrison of Fort II is not known.

CORBRIDGE UNDER HADRIAN

In AD 122 the emperor Hadrian decided to strengthen and supplement the Stanegate frontier on the Tyne–Solway isthmus with his great wall, which he built 2.5 miles north of Corbridge. It was once thought that Corbridge was abandoned after the new forts were built along Hadrian's Wall in about AD 124, but there is no evidence for this: in fact Corbridge was modified at this time (Fort III). The *principia* was given its stone shrine or *aedes* (see page 6), the granaries were moved to the east side of the fort, and the barracks were rebuilt. What military unit was present at the time, however, is not known.

CORBRIDGE UNDER ANTONINUS PIUS

In AD 138 Hadrian died and his successor, Antoninus Pius, reversed his frontier policy in Britain, determining to advance into Scotland once more to build a frontier wall considerably further north, between the Forth and Clyde. As a rearward base on Dere Street, the main route north, Corbridge became the scene of frantic activity. The fort was rebuilt (Fort IVA) within the existing turf rampart. For the first time stone was used extensively in the main buildings; the barracks and defences were still of timber. Antoninus' governor in Britain from AD 139 to 142, Quintus Lollius Urbicus, is named on two magnificent panels (see page 15), dated to AD 139 and 140, which adorned the two new granaries (not those seen today).

The Antonine Wall in Scotland was short-lived, a venture frustrated by military emergencies on the Continent and rebellion in the Scottish Lowlands. By AD 158 Hadrian's Wall was already being recommissioned and the withdrawal of the army from Scotland had begun, to be completed on Antoninus' death in AD 161. An inscription shows that some soldiers of the 6th Legion (see below) were stationed at Corbridge in about AD 158. In or shortly after 161 the auxiliary unit *Cohors I Vardullorum* (originally raised in northern Spain) dedicated an inscription at Corbridge. At about this time the last major modifications were made to the fort (Fort IVB), including the rebuilding of the barracks in stone.

A LEGIONARY BASE AND TOWN DEVELOP

In the early AD 160s the function of Corbridge suddenly changed to that of a base for legionaries. The auxiliary unit *Cohors I Vardullorum* was transferred elsewhere. Two important inscriptions show that Corbridge was now home to detachments from the 20th Legion (*Legio XX Valeria Victrix*) whose main base was at Chester near north Wales and the 6th Legion (*Legio VI Victrix*) from York. The layout of the living quarters for the legionaries in this period is not clearly understood, but was within the area of the old fort.

Above: Cavalry parade helmet from Newstead fort, which from AD 160 to 180 was supported by legionary troops sent up from their base at Corbridge

These legionary detachments had more wide-ranging duties than their auxiliary predecessors. They sent troops from their Corbridge base to help man a chain of outpost forts that lay beyond Hadrian's Wall along Dere Street as far as Newstead on the river Tweed. They also oversaw Corbridge as a supply depot and market for the northern frontier, a role well suited to its position at an intersection of road and river routes.

Rebuilding at Corbridge

Building fragments and a dedication of the AD 160s by the 6th Legion, found reused in the later town, are the earliest evidence for temples at Corbridge. They probably came from a sanctuary of classical temples (see page 27), outside the centre of the site. The 160s is likely to be when the bridge across the Tyne was rebuilt as a magnificent stone structure of at least six arches and when the granaries, too, were rebuilt.

Shorden Brae Mausoleum

Little is known about the cemeteries of Corbridge, but cremations line Dere Street 400m north of the early forts, and another burial ground lay near the Stanegate 700m west of the site, in the area known as Shorden Brae. In 1958 foundations of a mausoleum 10m² within an area some 40m² enclosed by a precinct wall were excavated.

The remains, dating from the second half of the second century, were all that survived of a massive tomb in the form of an elaborate tower.

Various ornate architectural fragments reused in the Saxon church at Hexham (visible in the crypt and walls; see page 46), were almost certainly taken from the monument, and give an idea of its scale and appearance. They include parts of giant fluted pilasters once over 5m high, a rosette panel, richly carved friezes, and part of a decorated open arch from an upper stage.

The mausoleum held an empty grave and a number of later burials were clustered around the monument.

The tomb has no parallel in Britain and is one of the largest tower tombs known from the Roman world. The high-ranking official for whom it must have been built remains a mystery, although it may have been for the governor or legionary commander known to have been killed in the invasion of AD 180 or 181 that is thought to have breached the Wall near Corbridge.

Left: A Roman tower tomb of the mid third century at Igel, Germany. The tomb at Corbridge would have been a similarly elaborate, but taller, structure

Below: A rosette panel from the Shorden Brae tomb, displayed in the nave wall of Hexham church

Site XI, thought to have been a combined warehouse and *macellum* (market), was probably also begun in the 160s, or perhaps in the following decade. But it was never completed. Building work stopped suddenly before even the foundations of the northern range were laid. A distinctive layer of burnt clay from superstructures of timber buildings ('the Corbridge destruction deposit'), was found overlying the unfinished foundations – evidence that a destructive fire, perhaps the result of enemy attack, destroyed much of the centre of Corbridge. Before the fire the ramparts of the old fort had been levelled and overlain by buildings, showing that a town had already begun to develop.

The Empire at War

Although it is not known whether it was the fire that brought the legionary builders of Site XI to a halt, or whether work had already stopped, these decades were a time of crisis. The Continental empire was ravaged by war and plague in the later 160s and troops had to be transferred from Britain at short notice. The historian Cassius Dio records a serious breach of Hadrian's Wall by invaders from the north in AD 180 or 181, which led to the 'greatest war' of Commodus' reign taking place in Britain. It is possible that it was during this invasion that Corbridge was burnt.

Many of the timber buildings destroyed in the fire may have belonged to traders and merchants attached to the legionary base at Corbridge and forming part of its civilian community. Corbridge was already acquiring the character of a town at this time and may even have been given official status as a *civitas* capital (a regional capital) when the old fort defences were finally removed some time before the AD 180s.

Above: Reconstruction of the temple dedicated to Sol Invictus in about AD 163, from fragments found used in the rebuilding of the Stanegate

'The greatest war was the one in Britain. When the tribes of the island, crossing the wall that separated them from the Roman legions, proceeded to commit many outrages and cut down a general together with his soldiers, Commodus was seized with fear and sent Ulpius Marcellus against them' Historian Cassius Dio writing of his contemporary the emperor Commodus, who is depicted on the coin above of AD 184–5. The reverse reads VICT[ORIAE] BRIT[ANNICAE], 'For victory in Britain'

Above: Portrait bust of Septimius
Severus from the early third century,
by which time he had restored peace
on the northern frontier in Britain
Below: Iron knife with a bone handle
and a pair of bronze shears found at
Corbridge, and probably produced
there in one of the many workshops
of the Roman town

Right: Reconstruction of Corbridge
town at its most extensive, c. AD 225

A The Stanegate

B Dere Street enters town, south

C Dere Street enters town, north

D Courtyard building, Site XI
   (probable marketing centre)

E East legionary compound

F West legionary compound

G Shops or storehouses (probable)

H Civilian houses and workshops

I Granaries

J Fountain

K *Mansio* (posting inn), or
   high-status house

L High-status house (conjectural)

M Baths and temple enclave
   (conjectural)

N Bridge over the Tyne

O The Cor Burn

THE THIRD AND FOURTH CENTURIES
The Legionary Compounds

In the early third century, after the emperor Septimius Severus
(r. AD 192–211) had restored stability to the province and its
northern frontier (see box page 44), Corbridge remained a
legionary base. The central part of the site now achieved its
visible layout, with the building of special walled compounds
for two legionary units. Inscriptions suggest that in the third
century these detachments were drawn from the 2nd Legion
(*Legio II Augusta*), based at Caerleon, south Wales, and from
either the 6th Legion or more probably the 20th Legion.
Detachments of the 2nd and 20th legions were also garrisoned
together at Carlisle in the third century.

   At this time, under Septimius Severus, the granaries were
completed in their visible and enormous form. The fountain
and public water supply that links to the compounds is
probably of the same period.

   By the early 200s, if not before, an extensive civilian town
had grown up around the core of the legionary garrison and
supply depot. The walls around the legionary compounds are

meandering and their gates ornate rather than defensive, suggesting that their main function was to separate the military community from a substantial surrounding civilian population.

The Civilian Life

The streets of the town extend into the fields outside the modern enclosure. Aerial photographs and the Edwardian excavation plan show that these streets were lined with strip-houses, long half-timbered buildings with narrow street frontages where shops jostled for the trade of passing customers. The inhabitants would have been manufacturers and traders in foodstuffs, pottery, glass, iron and cast bronze items, jewellery, textiles, leather and providers of services – everything from medicine to innkeeping.

A community of immigrant civilian traders (a *vicus*) was found at every Roman fort in the third century, since the free market was the main instrument of army supply. But in the fourth century army supply became a centralized state function, and most of the fort *vici* were abandoned. Corbridge and Carlisle, however, had become established civilian towns, no

Above: *Metalwork from Corbridge, dating from the second century* AD

A Gold and silver *fibula* (brooch), used to fasten clothing

B Bronze fretwork belt plate

C Bronze and enamel cockerel

Above: A Celtic head, probably representing a god, from Corbridge. Indigenous beliefs retained a place in the life of the town

longer reliant on their origins as military supply bases, and they continued to prosper in the late Roman period, the only substantial civilian settlements near the Wall.

The Settled Community

Corbridge must have become a social centre where families and dependants of soldiers based at other forts lived once their *vici* were abandoned, and where some rich inhabitants chose to settle. Two epitaphs show that the population included veterans. The town also appears to have attracted increasing numbers of the indigenous population, as evidenced by the finds indicating Celtic influence (see pages 25 and 32). But we have little evidence for the identities or lives of the late Roman population because the practice of erecting stone inscriptions had largely ceased by the mid third century.

Septimius Severus: an African Emperor in Britain

Septimius Severus (AD 145–211), from modern Libya, seized control of the Empire in AD 192, capturing Britain from his rival Albinus in 197. In 208 Severus, aged 63, but 'in his heart more enthusiastic than any youth', according to the historian Herodian, set out for Britain to campaign north of Hadrian's Wall. With him travelled his wife, Julia Domna, his elder son and co-emperor, Caracalla, his younger son, Geta, and the whole of the imperial court. For three years the Empire was ruled from Britain while a vast army invaded and ravaged south-east Scotland.

Corbridge was one of two main supply bases for these operations. The other lay to the east at South Shields at the mouth of the Tyne, from where supplies were shipped north. From Corbridge supplies and troops went north by road (Dere Street).

There is evidence that Severus toured the forts of the Wall area, inspecting the work on the frontier that he had ordered before his great invasion of the north. Certainly he will have inspected the granaries at Corbridge, rebuilt for the *expeditio felicissima Britannica*, 'the most fortunate British expedition'.

Faced with a guerrilla war in difficult terrain, even the celebrated Roman army was unable to win a decisive victory in Scotland. Seething with frustration, the aged Severus died in York in 211. His sons, who had no interest in pursuing the British venture to completion, returned with their father's ashes to Rome, and Britain slipped once more out of the imperial limelight.

Above: Septimius Severus, his wife, Julia Domna, and their sons, Caracalla and Geta (whose face has been removed – after his murder by his brother). The painting dates from about AD 200

Left: Altar from Corbridge to an unknown god, mentioning the 'most fortunate British expedition' – probably that of Severus in AD 209–11

Corbridge was probably capital of a self-governing administrative division, or *civitas* (as was Carlisle in the west). A tribal name was added to the place name Coria, but the combination only survives in corrupt forms ('Corstopitum' and 'Corie Lopocarium') in later Roman sources. In the fourth century the town was apparently surrounded by a defensive wall. There may still have been a military presence here (as in fourth-century Carlisle) in the compounds at the centre of the town, but the identity of any late Roman garrison is unknown.

THE ROMANS LEAVE

Major centrally organized building works took place as late as 370, but Corbridge seems to have been rapidly abandoned when Roman administration in Britain collapsed in the early years of the fifth century. By about 600 the Saxons had settled half a mile east of the Roman town, at a good fording place. By this time the Roman bridge must have been unusable, but striking enough a ruin to lend its name to the successor settlement, modern Corbridge. The Roman site was known in the Middle Ages and later variously as Corchester or Colchester. All these names derive from the Roman Coria.

For centuries the ruins of Roman Corbridge were a quarry for stone-robbers. King John dug for treasure here in 1201, finding nothing but stones 'marked with brass, iron and lead' – blocks, like those in the fountain, bonded with metal cramps.

The 16th-century antiquaries John Leland and William Camden were struck by the upstanding remains, and even in 1725 Roger Gale described 'the circuit of the walls' as visible. The site was levelled by agricultural work in about 1810.

Above: The antiquarian William Camden (1551–1623) was struck by the remains at Corbridge; portrait by Marcus Gheeraerts the Younger, 1609
Below: Corbridge altar discovered in 1754, dedicated in Greek to the eastern goddess Astarte (see box page 26); drawing, published in 1773

The Corbridge Lanx

'Isabell Cutter, daughter of Thomas Cutter of Corbridge, blacksmith, aged nine years … did on or about the tenth day of February last past find an ancient silver piece of plate in a great measure covered with the earth, one end sticking out of the ground, at a certain place within this manor near the north bank of the river Tyne by the water edge'
Excerpt of a court leet ruling in May 1735, on the ownership of the lanx

Right: The Corbridge Lanx. Apollo stands (right) before a shrine holding his bow, his lyre at his feet. Standing with her hand raised in conversation is Athena, talking to Artemis (left), twin sister of Apollo. In the foreground Artemis' hunting dog, a fallen stag and a griffin flank an altar. The other two women may be Leto (seated), mother of the twins, and her sister Ortygia, who was transformed into the island of Delos, on which this scene is set.

Above: Finial (decorative top) to a section of the Roman bridge that crossed the Tyne just south-west of Corbridge

THE FIRST EXCAVATIONS

In 1861–2 excavation by William Coulson uncovered the northern end of the Roman bridge and other structures inside the town. But the richness and extent of Roman Corbridge was only properly revealed in an ambitious excavation campaign during the summers of 1906–14, which as well as the central area explored the remains in the surrounding fields. The digging was on such a scale that a miniature railway was built to remove the spoil in wagons.

The first two seasons were supervised by Leonard Woolley, later famous as excavator of Ur in Mesopotamia, but

Hexham Abbey

There were still upstanding Roman buildings at Corbridge in about AD 674 when Saxon masons took stone to build the new church ordered by Wilfrid, Bishop of York at Hexham, three miles away. Of this church the crypt, which was rediscovered in 1725, survives. Many reused Roman stones can still be seen in the crypt, including blocks with tooled decoration from the bridges at Corbridge and Chesters, and ornate architectural fragments, such as parts of giant fluted pilasters that probably came

from the tower tomb at Shorden Brae (see page 40).

Inscriptions, too, survive: a fragment of a dedication to Apollo Maponus that was cut down to form the lintel of a door in the crypt, and a slab marking the building of the granaries under Septimius Severus (see page 13).

Of the many other Roman stones in the abbey church, the most striking is the tombstone of the standard-bearer Flavinus. It stands 2.64m high and shows the mounted cavalryman, with plumed helmet and standard, trampling a hirsute barbarian.

Left: This second- or third-century relief of Jupiter from Corbridge, now in Hexham Abbey, had been used in the building of the Saxon church

Above: Part of the crypt at Hexham Abbey, its walls partly built of stones from Corbridge

Below: Watercolour of a chamber of the crypt at Hexham, by Henry Richardson, c.1850. The decorated Roman stones can be clearly seen

Above: Brooches excavated at Corbridge, dating (from left to right) from the fourth, second and third centuries AD
Left: Excavations at Corbridge in 1909. The little railway was used to remove excavated material

at Corbridge he was still utterly inexperienced. He later confessed: 'I had never so much as seen an excavation, I had never studied archaeological methods, even from books … I had no qualifications at all'. After Woolley's departure for Egypt in 1907 the excavations were run by a native of Corbridge, Robert Forster, a barrister, novelist and Captain of the Thames Rowing Club, and Henry Knowles, a local architect, who produced the excellent survey plans.

None of these excavations was conducted using archaeological techniques that we would use today, but the 1906–14 campaign was well recorded and published by the standards of the time. The reports are still a rich source of information for the whole site and, apart from air photography, the only source for the extensive later Roman town. The work was recorded in a series of photographs which shows the people involved – local workmen and volunteers as well as the supervisors – and which constitutes a remarkable social document on archaeological methods in Edwardian England.

Above: Leonard Woolley (right) with TE Lawrence at Ur, Mesopotamia, in the 1920s. Woolley ran the excavations at Corbridge from 1906–7
Below left: The granaries under excavation in 1909
Below: Robert Forster in 1910 packing up an inscription at Corbridge, where he ran the excavations after Woolley

Right: The Durham University Corbridge training dig on a field trip in 1951. John Gillam (seated front, with glasses) was Ian Richmond's co-director and the leading excavator at Corbridge after Richmond's departure. Norman McCord (second from right), was later present at the finding of the Corbridge Hoard
Below: Bronze enamelled vase, one of the grave goods from a cremation cemetery along the line of Dere Street that was discovered in 1974 during creation of the new A69 bypass
Bottom: View of Corbridge today, looking north-east over the remains of the fountain on the Stanegate towards Site XI

CORBRIDGE TODAY

The First World War brought the annual excavations to an end. In 1933 the central part of the site, containing the most important excavated buildings, was given to the nation by HD Cuthbert. Smaller excavations were carried out here almost every year from 1934, and from 1947–73 an annual training dig, concentrating on the early forts, was run by the Universities of Durham and Newcastle. This 'Corbridge School' produced a generation of Hadrian's Wall archaeologists and Roman army experts, inspired by the leaders in the Corbridge work: Eric Birley, Ian Richmond (until 1955) and, after the Second World War, John Gillam. In 1974 a road scheme revealed the Red House fort and a cemetery along Dere Street (see page 35 and box page 40). The last excavation was in 1980, on the site of the new museum.

Today the central area is in the care of English Heritage. The visible remains are largely those uncovered before 1914; the outlying parts of the site were backfilled. Our knowledge of the early forts is incomplete, and the civilian settlements attached to those forts, and much of the later legionary compounds and town, lie unexplored in the surrounding fields. Despite the many distinguished archaeologists who have wrestled with the problems of Corbridge since 1906, there is much about this beguiling place that is still to be discovered.